WHEN A BOOK IS A GOLD MINE:

The Entrepreneur's Shortcut To Market Domination

By

Travis Cody

Travis Cody
Visit the Official Travis Cody Website at:
www.TravisCody.com

Printed in the United States of America

First Printing: March 2016

Axios Publishing

ISBN: 978-0-692-62045-8

Axios Publishing books may be purchased for educational, business or sales promotional use. Special discounts are available on quantity purchases. For more information, please call or write.

Telephone: (323) 325-5456;
Email: sales@axiospublishing.com

For orders by U.S. trade bookstores and wholesalers, please contact Axios Publishing at the phone or email address listed above.

DISCLAIMER

The Publisher has strived to be as accurate and complete as possible in the creation of this book.

This book is not intended for use as a source of legal, business, accounting or financial advice. All readers are advised to seek services of competent professionals in legal, business, accounting, and finance field.

In practical advice books, like anything else in life, there are no guarantees of income made. Readers are cautioned to rely on their own judgment about their individual circumstances to act accordingly.

While all attempts have been made to verify information provided in this publication, the Publisher assumes no responsibility for errors, omissions, or contrary interpretation of the subject matter herein. Any perceived slights of specific persons, peoples, or organizations are unintentional.

TABLE OF CONTENTS

FOREWORD
BY
JAMES SHRAMKO,
Founder of SuperFastBusiness.com

It's a rare opportunity to share a private beach house in Malibu CA for three days with a dozen other 7-figure entrepreneurs.

I had traveled from Australia just for this event and was the keynote speaker. It's always humbling to have very successful entrepreneurs listening to your own way of doing things. After all – they're already successful. You really do need to be confident in what you're doing!

Over the course of three days every marketing strategy and method these successful business people were using was discussed, analyzed, torn down and then rebuilt into something better.

It was an incredible information exchange between the best marketers of the world in what works right now.

While everyone in the room was successful in their own right, one man had something that everyone wanted: How to become a bestselling author. (Even a world famous copywriter, inquired about his service!)

I knew immediately that Travis Cody had struck business gold.

I learned that Travis had three #1 Bestselling books of his own. (This book will most likely make four!) Here was a man who walked the walk. Many of the questions he was asked had to do with the clients he had helped create bestselling books for.

Dozens personally; **Over 400** with the team that he works with. In practically every industry you can think of. Even more astonishing was that he has a 100% track record.

Obviously this fellow knew what he was doing. Yet what really intrigued me was what he did *after* the books became bestsellers.

You see, for Travis a bestselling book is just the start. He outlined the principles he used to then help his clients turn their book into profitable income streams.

He also made a very compelling argument that NOW was the best time in history for every business owner to have a book of their own.

Over lunch I listened in as the other marketers quizzed him, trying to extract as much information from him as they could. I was amused to hear his tale of how he discovered this process when ghostwriting a book for a drug dealer. (Fortunately for you, dear reader, you can create your own bestselling book with no risk to your kneecaps. And you'll read this amusing story for yourself shortly).

What was most shocking to me... (as someone who would rather talk than type...) was how easy it is for you to create a bestselling book. Most of us wrongly assume that writing a book is a tedious labor of love that takes years. Yet, here was a man who shared with us how to do it in under 6-weeks.

As you are about to discover, Amazon has created a platform that is a game changer when it comes to publishing a book. They have broken the centuries old publishing model of needing an agent, a publisher, and editor and a publicist – and made it possible for anyone to create a best-selling book.

This means that YOU can become the go-to expert in your field. And, depending on how you position yourself after the book comes out, you may also experience the perks of being a celebrity and well-known figure in your industry.

So is this book worth the read for you? In a word: YES.

As founder of SuperFastBusiness.com, I have helped thousands of business owners in dozens of industries find success online. The #1 challenge for the great bulk of them has been to find easy to understand, actionable guidelines and roadmaps.

If you've dreams of becoming a bestselling author... more importantly... making money with your book, *When A Book Is A Gold Mine* is exactly what you are looking for. Travis lays down the tracks to getting started in as simple as fashion as possible.

In all the business books I have read over the years, this book has the most actionable steps. This is not the fluff, the what or the why followed by endless case studies that push you to sign up for a seminar.

This book is the HOW.

The exact steps that anyone can follow to quickly create a book and push it onto the bestseller list.

Frankly, *When A Book Is A Gold Mine* sets the bar for highly-executable information that will result in you being able to make a big impact in your life and your business. Travis is the new style of educator who has already mapped a path for you.

This book will get you to success faster. Go get it!

CHAPTER 1

It Starts With a Book

I n the economy today, it's no longer enough to rely on traditional marketing methods to grow you business. Indeed, even the idea of the "traditional business" is slowly becoming quaint. How do we even define the term?

For purposes of this book, lets define it as a brick and mortar store or a service-based business where you provide a product or service. In this type of business, you advertise, clients come in, you sell them a product or service and they pay you.

This has been the modus operandi for thousands of years and continues to be the primary driver of economic growth the world over. However, in today's vastly connected world, this appears to no longer be enough for the small business owner. Especially if you want to achieve the type of financial growth and time freedom that you desire and deserve.

The business climate has changed drastically in the past decade. We have come out of the information era and are now squarely in the social media era. The world today is more connected than ever before. As such, we are attracted to the types of people, events and circumstances that support our value system and view of the world.

In a service-based business you can do perfectly well by serving one-time clients. If you're a dentist, clients come in, you clean their teeth, fix a cavity or two and they move on. If you're personable and you have an aggressive marketing program, you can follow up with them and get them to come back every six months for additional service. You build rapport and loyalty to create a stable foundation for your business.

Yet for most service-based businesses many clients are one-time only clients; they come in, they get the service, and they move on.

Throw in today's world of Groupon and LivingSocial deals and suddenly you have a formula for no loyalty for local business. If you can get a Groupon for a $20 teeth cleaning at five different dentists, why not just go to a different one each time?

This mix of hyper-competition and disappearing customer loyalty is one of the main reasons that "business as usual" is no longer enough.

You even see this problem with the bigger brands today. In the 80s, marketing efforts were focused on creating brand loyalty. If somebody was a Co-ca-Cola fan, they'd be with Coca-Cola forever. If they were a Ford person, they wouldn't drive anything that wasn't built by Ford. If they were a Gap person, they wouldn't go to Old Navy. They would stay loyal to Gap.

Yet that's no longer the case, especially with people under 30 (the Millennial Generation). To these buyers, it's always about the best deal. If you can get a tee shirt that looks exactly the same for half the price you'll go for cheaper tee shirt.

Because of this lack of brand loyalty the challenge for today's entrepreneurs and business owners is to increase the competitive advantage of your business.

The single most effective way you can do this is by "growing your celebrity" in your marketplace to become the go-to, definitive choice. When you do this you can literally double the revenue of your company without having to provide any additional services.

Sounds great, doesn't it? Well, the best part is that this can all be done through the creation of one simple book. And today I will show you why having a book is so important for your business.

Better yet, I will show you an extremely simple way for you to create one in in a few short hours.

Everyone Can Be an Author

Every business needs a book, and here's why: It used to be that the most authority and credibility came from someone who had a PhD, an MD or some other advanced education. Yet that's no longer the case.

We're now in a time where consumers are more likely to listen to a celebrity than a scientist. For instance, imagine a PhD from MIT is having a debate with Tom Cruise about global warming. If the doctor is dreadfully boring, dry, and speaks in a monotone voice, while Tom Cruise is very animated and passionate about what he does, then you will remember more of Tom Cruise's comments.

When a Book Is a Gold Mine

I'm not saying you will agree with Tom Cruise. You may actually think he's an idiot. Yet you will remember his point of view.

And even though the you may agree with the scientist's viewpoint, if he is boring, chances are you will tune out what he says as you go watch Funny Cat videos.

With celebrity, it's not necessarily about being right. *It's about being remembered* and being someone who can command attention.

In a similar way, the advantage of having a book is this: You, as a business owner, can actually create credibility, authority, and *celebrity* in your marketplace so people will want to hear what you have to say. And it's even better because you actually are right!

This point was driven home very powerfully about a year ago. I was watching the news and Deepak Chopra was on CNN commenting on a current event.

When Dr. Chopra first published his books he made a big splash on the scene and started to become a celebrity in his own right.

At that time, whenever he was on TV the footer that told who he was always said "Dr. Deepak Chopra, MD". When I saw him on CNN in this more recent instance he was there commenting on something that was outside of his field of expertise.

The thing that struck me though was that the footer didn't say Dr. Deepak Chopra. It didn't say Deepak Chopra, MD. It said Deepak Chopra, *Bestselling Author.*

Think about that: in today's business environment and in today's world in general being *a bestselling author has more credibility than being a doctor!*

This is extraordinary. Over the last hundred years when polls were taken to ask, "Who's the most trusted professional?" it has always been a doctor.

As I learned on CNN that day, this would appear to no longer be the case.

When a Book Is a Gold Mine

Traditionally, the amount of time, effort, money, planning and coordination to achieve the "best selling author" badge has been impossible for most.

To start with, it required that you find a publisher who would print your book in the first place. An almost impossible task in and of itself.

However, in the early 2000's the game changed when Jeff Bezos, the Founder of Amazon, launched Amazon Publishing. Bezos had a vision to help more people become authors. He thought that the publishing industry was antiquated, prehistoric and that there was a better way to do things.

He knew that there were a lot of people in the world who had enough experience for a book. Yet the traditional publishing industry was so entrenched in their ways they made it nearly impossible for anyone to share their voice.

As you can imagine, (or may remember) the response from the publishing industry was not a positive one. In effect, they said, "We're gonna sue you. That's not fair. You're a book distributor; you can't be a publisher too."

Of course, this was total hypocrisy because most of the publishing companies were part of conglomerates that also owned distribution channels, bookstores, etc.

In any event, Bezos eventually backed down and canceled his plans for a publishing company.

The publishing industry declared it a huge victory and felt they had showed that upstart online book guy what was what.

Only three years later Jeff Bezos introduced a new gadget called the Kindle. He also announced "I'm gonna let anybody publish a book. Plus, they can publish it for free."

The response from the book industry was less than enthusiastic, as can be imagined. Publishing experts proclaimed "What a joke. Electronic books will never go anywhere."

Less than four years later and Borders went insolvent and shut down. Most other bookstores were severely struggling to stay afloat.

When a Book Is a Gold Mine

Jeff Bezos gutted the industry through innovation. He brought something new to the market that had been needed and wanted for a long time. A milestone was reached: *now anyone can become an author.*

This is good news for you. Amazon, with the Kindle and their CreateSpace arm, has made it possible for anyone to be able to share his or her voice.

And I am here to tell you that everyone has a book inside of them. Indeed, this has created a new breed of business people: the *Authorpreneur*. These are people who use books to grow their business, their brand and their income.

Anyone who has a hobby that they love; anyone who has been in a job for more than four or five years; anyone who is a parent; anyone who has a special skill or talent; and especially anyone who is an entrepreneur or owns their own business has a book inside of them.

Now, I want to stop right here and acknowledge that the idea of writing a book may terrify you.

You may have been horrible in English. In school, you may have hated writing. You may have been mocked or ridiculed for the things you wrote. (Ok, that was *my* experience. Perhaps you can relate).

Or you may simply feel "There's no way I could ever do that. That's just way too big for me."

I used to think the same thing. Yet with this book I am now a four-time best selling author with three #1 titles to my credit. And by knowing the rapid writing system and bestseller marketing strategies I am about to teach you, that number will only grow in the coming years.

I promise you, *creating a book is much easier than you think*. And I will show you the easy way to do it. I'm not even going to say that I will show you how to "write a book" because there are ways to share your voice, your experience, your expertise and your knowledge that require very little writing from you personally.

Ways that don't involve hiring expensive ghostwriters either.

When a Book Is a Gold Mine

If you:

- Have a hobby that you love...

- Have been at your job for two years or more...

- Are a parent...

- Have a special skill or talent...

- Are an Entrepreneur...

- Own your own business...

- Have read more than three books on one topic...

Then you have a book inside you that is just waiting to be written and published.

CHAPTER 2

The Movie-Star Method for Writing a Book:

How Anyone Can Go From Blank Page to Published Author in 6 Weeks or Less

Yes, it really is possible to write your book in six weeks or less. I know... six weeks sounds pretty ludicrous to most people. Yet I have a client who actually created his last book in a single day. (Many clients finish in less than 4 weeks.)

When we start the process many of my clients are skeptical to be sure.

They feel it's going to be too hard and too laborious. Or they think they're not a good writer and it's going to suck. And perhaps this is what's going through your mind right now as well.

The great news for you is that there are much more effective ways to get your expertise out of your noggin' and onto the page other than you just pecking away at the keyboard one key at a time.

And the most sure-fire way is the "Movie Star Method" of writing books.

My clients who have gone through this process are able to finish the first draft of their book in less than two weeks. And they are able to do that without investing more than 10 hours of their personal time during the entire process.

I am sure that as a successful entrepreneur, parent, or hobbyist you may be thinking: "There's no way I have enough time to write a book."

Yet have you ever wondered how someone who is always on set making a movie finds the time to write and publish a book? Or someone who runs a country? (After all, if they're running a country, when do they have time to write?)

It's simple.

They have knowledge, interesting stories and experience in what they're doing. They want to share their unique perspective about the world in a way that will outlive them. But how do they do it?

Here's the secret: rather than sitting down in front of a blank computer screen and typing, they simply hire someone to interview them.

The process works like this:

Step 1: "Author" is interviewed.

Step 2: Interviews are transcribed.

Step 3: Transcriptions are sent to an editor who cleans them up.

Step 4: Edited manuscript is organized and outlined into a logical flow

Step 5: 2nd edit for grammar

Step 6: Manuscript sent out to graphic designer to be laid out

Step 7: Book Cover is created

Step 8: Publish

In a nutshell, that's how the majority of famous people get their book written.

Take, for example, Arnold Schwarzenegger's book *Total Recall: My Unbelievably True Life Story*. In the acknowledgements he directly states that the book was created from about 50 hours of interviews where Arnold sat down and had a conversation about his life.

Now that you know how it works, you are going to follow that same process and be the movie star of your own life.

And to make even easier, I'm going to share a few different ways for you to structure your book since this is not a "one size fits all" system.

Find the approach that works the best for you and then do that. The idea here is to keep it as easy and as simple as possible.

Rapid Writing Method #1: One Problem, One Solution

The first way to write a book quickly and easily is to follow the "One problem, One solution" process.

First, take some time to brainstorm the struggles that you customers face. A great way to keep yourself focused is to start with the title of your book.

A quick technique you can use is the guidebook technique.

For example: Complete Guide to _____.

If you're a Real Estate Agent, you could create a _Complete Guide to Buying Your First Home._ Or a _Complete Guide to Selling Your House in a Slow Market._

If you're a Dentist: _Complete Guide to All Natural Tooth Care_

Now, just take that topic and break it into three or four core problems. Each one of these will be a chapter.

For the Real Estate Agent and First Time Homebuyer guide you could have:

Chapter 1: 10 Things Every First Time Homebuyer Absolutely Has to Know

Chapter 2: How to Find the Perfect Mortgage for Your Unique Situation

Chapter 3: Ninja Negotiation Strategies That Ensure You Get the Best Price

Chapter 4: The Top 5 Traps to Look For When Viewing A House

These are usually all of the things that you personally are aware of and are familiar with when it comes to that problem.

Now, when outlining your chapters just answer questions that solve the problem that you or your product/service solves.

For Example:

1. What are the common obstacles that prevent customers from achieving the out come they want? (Lack of knowledge? Lack of the right Tools? Poor Mindset?)

2. What are the most common fears that customers have when striving for the outcome they want? (Failing? Being embarrassed? Losing money?)

3. What common misinformation might be holding your customer back?

4. What are some of the unknown obstacles or pitfalls they need to be aware of? (What do you know as the expert that they don't know?)

Rapid Writing Method #2: The Answer to All Your Questions

If you deal with clients directly, then I'm sure you get asked questions all the time. And many of them are probably the same question over and over again. There's even a term for it: frequently asked questions.

Yet, ask yourself, how much time do you waste answering these same questions again and again? What if there was a way you could answer all those frequently asked questions just *once* so that you can get right to the business of serving you customer? Lucky for you, there is.

Step 1: Set a timer for 20 minutes.

Step 2: Turn off all distractions. Shut down your Internet browsers, turn off your Facebook messenger and put your phone on silent so it's not pinging you.

You want to be totally focused on this one task for twenty minutes.

Step 3: Start the timer and for 20 minutes write down all of the most frequenlty asked questions that you get asked in your business. Don't edit and don't censor yourself. Just write down as many as you can think of in 20 minutes.

At the end of 20 minutes STOP. Get up and walk around for 5-10 minutes, get a drink of water, etc. After your short break come back, set the timer for another 20 minutes and then repeat the process again.

Repeat this process for as many times as you can until you just can't think of any more frequently asked questions to write down. At first you may only have 30 questions. However, the more you times you do this, the more you are going to come up with. I've had clients that have gotten as many as 200 questions after only two writing sessions.

Another thing you can also do is to take your list and show it to your staff. Ask them, "Are there any questions that our customers ask you that aren't on this list?" Have them write down their questions and then add them to your list.

Once you're finished, you'll repeat the exercise only this time you're going to write down all of the "should ask" questions. These are all of those things that your customer doesn't know that they don't know.

If you're a Real Estate Agent and you're dealing with a first time homebuyer they may ask you all of the standard questions they found online about square footage, year built, cost of utilities, etc.

Yet what they should be asking you are detailed questions about the types of materials used to build the house, if the house ever had any water damage, how old the roof is, etc. So write them all down.

Now that you have your two lists go through and organize the questions into groups that relate to each other together.

For example, if you're a Real Estate Agent then you may have a dozen or more questions that are just about financing a home; or how to sell a house quickly; or things that new home buyers should look out for.

By organizing similar questions together you are forming a basic outline for your book.

Rapid Writing Method #3: I Don't Have a Lot of Time Method

This is by the fastest method for getting your book created. It does have the downside of possibly creating a book with the least amount of your voice in it.

Step 1: Write down 10 topics/areas about your business. If you're a dentist, for example, some of those topics could be: teeth cleaning, teeth whitening, braces, braces versus Invisalign, toothpaste (types of toothpastes, and which is better), toothbrushes, etc.

Step 2: Write 10 facts about each one of those topics.

Step 3: Write one sentence about each of these facts.

With that, you've just created an outline for your book. Each of the ten topics is a chapter, and underneath each chapter, there are 10 facts. Each one of those facts is a subhead of the chapter and you have the first sentence for each fact.

Step 4: Send this outline to a ghostwriter and have them fill in the rest of the book. Since you've already written the first sentence for each sub-heading, the ghostwriter will know what they're to write about.

You've got the topics, you've got the facts, and you've got a paragraph to get them started. With a little research, a decent ghostwriter will be able to fill in all of the rest, and you will have a book.

Right now, take a minute to think about how many topics you have in your business.

How many books could you create from those?

You'll soon see that you have more than one book worth of experience and expertise to share.

Now you just have to get all your knowledge out and onto the page.

Now The Fun Part: The Interview.

Relax. The hard part of creating your book is finished! Regardless of which method you chose to follow to create your book, you're practically home free at this point.

Now it's time to have some fun.

Take the questions or topics that you have written and set up a time to be interviewed. There are several ways to do this. Again, just choose the one that suits you best.

The easiest way to do the interview is to get a voice recorder or to use the recorder on your phone and start answering the questions that you just wrote down. Just imagine that you are having a conversation with a close friend and he or she is asking the questions.

If it seems awkward or strange for you to talk to yourself, (oddly, I seem to have no problem with this!) have someone else interview you.

You can have your spouse, a friend, a co-worker or even an employee do the interview. Do what is most comfortable for you and that will give you the best chance of getting it done.

You may even want to treat this like a radio interview, which is good practice for all the ones you will do once your book comes out.

If you have yet to do any media appearances here's a little secret: They almost always ask you the questions you give them. Yep. On Radio and TV the people being interviewed are simply being asked questions that they already know the answer to... because they wrote them! That's why when you see an expert on TV they seem so polished and knowledgeable.

I'm "writing" this while driving in my car. I have a business appointment that is a two-hour drive each way. I turned my voice recorder on and I imagine that there is a good friend on the ride with me. We are having a very lovely conversation during which I am revealing all my secrets to him.

I've found that for most people the most difficult part in all of this is just getting started. The most common reason for not getting started is "I don't know what to talk about."

Yet, when I sit down and ask my clients to tell me the story of how they got into the business they're in, we end up having an hour-long conversation. That conversation alone is 30 pages of a book and that's just from us talking about how they got into business.

If I then ask about the things they really enjoy about their work, that's another 30-45 minute conversation and another 15-20 pages of their book.

So let me get you started with a few questions you can answer about YOUR business or service.

- How did you get into the business you're in?

- What do you enjoy about your job?

- What are the most exciting advances in your industry right now?

- What changes have you seen over the last few years?

- Based on your experience where do you think your industry will go next?

- What are some of the best experiences you've had with clients in your business?

- What has been some of the results that your clients have had?

- How have your clients lives been changed by the service that you offer?

Answer those and you have the introduction to your book finished.

I told you this was an easy process.

Now, answer your FAQ/SAQ's and you're practically finished.

That's it.

If you were able write over a 100 questions you have more than enough material for a book.

120 questions will take you around four hours to answer in an interview style discussion. My experience has shown that when you transcribe a 4-hour interview, you end up with about 90 pages (8.5 x 11) in a word document.

When you format that information for a 6 x 9, or 5.25 x 8 book, you end up with 160-200 pages, depending on how you space it. That is a very legitimate, nice-sized book.

I have a mentor who is one of the top 500 book reviewers on Amazon. He has dozens of books sent to him each week for his review. So many books are sent to him because his review carries so much weight on Amazon that it can boost the visibility of the book.

He told me that he has noticed a trend that has taken place over the last few years: Many of the most popular best-selling books are under 160 pages. So 160 pages is a great length to shoot for, especially if you only plan to release on Kindle.

If that seems like too much of a commitment for the first book, don't worry, that is how most people feel at this point.

The *One Problem, One Solution* process is a simple way to help you get started. It will help you create a short book in a short amount of time with little effort. And as you gain more confidence in the process, you can always go back and add to the books you have already written with new year editions or create new books altogether.

Congratulations! By the time you have finished just one of these exercises, 85% of your book is complete.

See How Easy That Was?

Now that you know the secret, just repeat the process to create multiple books and before you know it you'll be the dominant force in your industry.

Tim Ferriss was totally unknown until he released *The 4-Hour Workweek*. He leveraged a single book to create a mini-empire all his own.

Makayla Léone and Pamela Donnelly – two of my coaching clients - followed this exact process for their first book. (Both of which went on to become #1 Bestsellers.) They then leveraged those books to build thriving businesses.

And you can too.

I'll leave you with one last insider tip: When you create your first book you don't need to share 100% of everything you know. Break up your knowledge into multiple books.

For instance, going back to our Real Estate Agent from earlier: You can have a single book on *How to Finance Your Dream Home; The Top 25 Things to Look For When Buying a House* or even *Insider Secrets to Selling Your House Fast.*

This is the secret to being a multi-bestselling author.

However, you're not done yet. There are a few more steps to do first.

Yet before we get to those I would like to share an advanced marketing strategy with you.

How would you like to not only create your book, but also create a full years worth of content for your blog and social media at the same time?

It's completely possible. And when you master this, you will enter that rare arena of prolific content creators.

When a Book Is a Gold Mine

This is the secret to becoming the dominant force in your market.

And lucky for you, practically no one will do this because they feel it's too much work.

With this method, you're able to work once for a 10X return.

CHAPTER 3

Advanced Strategies:

How to Create a Year's Worth of Content in a Single Afternoon

When a Book Is a Gold Mine

This is an advanced strategy that I use with some of my clients. However, I must warn you, sometimes they get hung up on the process and it drastically slows down their progress.

If you're the type of person that feels, "Things have to be perfect, and I really need to look good at all times," then don't do this. Most likely you'll get hung up on the technical elements and never get anything done.

If you're the type of person that has an attitude of, "I kick ass. I can do anything that I want and my voice deserves to be heard. I deserve to be serving thousands, if not tens of thousands, if not hundreds of thousands or millions of people because what I know about my business is very valuable and can change lives," then you're going to love this method.

In the previous chapters you learned how to structure your book as a series of interviews.

The difference is that instead of recording the audio of you answering your questions, you will film yourself answering the questions one camera.

Now don't worry, this requires no film crew, make up artist, lights, or any technical equipment whatsoever.

If you have a cell phone, iPhone or tablet you have everything you need to create very high-quality videos.

All you have to do is sit at a desk or other nice location turn on your camera and start answering questions.

Most iPhones and mobile devices have tripods you can pick up for under $50.

The easiest way to make this work is to have a staff member, spouse or a friend sit just off camera. They read you a question. You look directly into the camera and repeat the question. Then, still looking directly into the camera, answer the question.

For example: If the question is, "Travis, what's the fastest way to create a book?" I would sit, look straight into the camera, and say "You know, many of my clients ask me, 'What's the fastest way to create a book?'" And then I would answer the question.

After you have answered the first question, the interviewer will ask you the second question. You repeat the question and then answer the question. Repeat this process for all the questions you have.

Most of my clients complete this process in a single afternoon (about 4-5 hours).

Congratulations, not only have you created your book in a single afternoon...You've also just created a year's worth of content.

Here's how:

Step 1: Take a copy of the video and get it transcribed.

Step 2: Send a copy of the video to a film editor and have them edit it so that each question/answer is its own short video. (Be sure to have a text overlay that references your website URL or Facebook page)

Step 3: Have the editor pull out the audio and create a separate mp3 audio file for each question/answer.

Depending on how many questions you came up with during the Chapter 2 exercises you will now have 100+ video and audio files of approximately 3-6 minutes each. (The length depends on how long it took you to answer each question. Obviously some questions will be more in-depth than others.)

Step 4: Take the transcription of each question and turn it into a PDF.

Step 5: Publish your videos to YouTube and other video sharing sites.

Step 6: Publish the transcription to your website as blog posts and publish to blog directories

Step 7: Submit the PDF's to article directories and sharing sites.

Step 8: Publish your audio files to iTunes as a podcast.

Can you see the power of this? In one single afternoon you created 100+ videos, audios, pdfs, and blog posts that you can publish through out the coming year.

If you only publish two podcasts, two videos, two blog posts and two PDF's a week you will have 50+ weeks of ongoing content.

And the best news is there are a lot of really powerful tools that allow you to schedule all of this in advance... *for the entire year*... all in one sitting.

You can even have one of your employee's upload all of this content into a service like Hootsuite or any of the other auto managers and the entire year's worth of content will go out automatically. You never have to do anything else.

And it gets even better. Because, as your content is spread across the Internet for a year your credibility will grow. Your social influence will grow. You'll start to get a lot of Google Love because you're content will be spread across multiple platforms.

Now you have all of this content and all of this critical mass growing behind you. And it only took you a single afternoon to make it all happen. How easy is that in today's crazy busy world?

For most people, when they think of a social media strategy… when they think of having to write blog posts… when they think about having to create videos… it's overwhelming.

A common response is "I simply do not have the time to do all that." Look, when it comes to social media and online marketing we all know we should be doing it but very few do. We don't do it because we convince ourselves we're too busy.

With this strategy you simply take a single day of your week, turn the camera on and stay there until all the questions you wrote are answered.

That's it.

And then you're done *for the entire year* in terms of creating content. Let somebody else handle all the editing and the uploading and the distribution of it.

When a Book Is a Gold Mine

Then, while that's being disseminated over the course of the year, you can spend time writing your second and third book following the same process.

By the end of the first year, you'll have years of social media and informational content loaded and ready to go.

CHAPTER 4

Editing:

How to Make Your Work Shine

When a Book Is a Gold Mine

First, you do have to make sure that your content is ready to go out into the world. The first step is to take your audio files and have them transcribed.

Transcription is really cheap. You can have it done for less than a dollar a minute. If you have a few hours of recording, you can get the transcription done for less than $200.

Once you have the transcription back you will have 85% of your book finished. All that needs to be done now is to take the rough material and edit it for grammar, structure, etc.

One thing you need to remember during this process is that you can't expect the transcriptions to be flawless. In fact, most likely you're going to read over the transcription and think, *"This can't be a book."*

This is because the way we speak and the way we write is slightly different. When you read the transcripts at first they are going to seem rough. That's why it's called a *rough draft*. That's why I say that your manuscript is only 85% finished at this point, and not 100%.

If you have reached this point, I would like to pause and say "Congratulations!" You have accomplished more than 99.9% of other people who want to write a book. Most people never even complete a rough draft.

Remember, at this point your draft is supposed to be rough and it's supposed to be ugly. It's not supposed to be pretty and polished. However, if you're very verbose and very eloquent in the way you communicate, your book may very well be 99% finished.

The thing to realize when writing a book is that you have to stop being focused on perfection. Stop being focused on, "This is my life's work, and this is my legacy."

That's not what we're creating with this. A definitive "legacy" book has its place and time. With your first book you're creating a branding tool. This tool will allow you to serve greater numbers of customers. It's a tool to establish yourself as the expert and the authority in your industry. You're creating your celebrity brand.

When a Book Is a Gold Mine

Now it's entirely possible that right now you're thinking *"Well, if the book is rough, how does that establish me as an authority, how does that make me a celebrity?"*

Here's a secret about celebrity branding: It's not the huge vocabulary or how polished your writing is that matters...*it's the information.*

And here's the other secret about publishing a book: 99% of the people you give the book to or who buy your book aren't going to read it. They'll read parts of it to be sure, but few will read it fully cover to cover.

Remember, you're creating this book to establish your credibility and your authority. I can't emphasize this enough.

I mention this because the #1 reason most people will never finish their book and the main reason that my clients take six months to get their book finished versus six weeks is because they get hung up on perfection.

Trust me, no matter how many times you edit the book, there's always something else that needs

to be fixed. With my first book I had three professional editors *plus* twelve of my closest friends
read the manuscript. Each one found errors that
were corrected.

When the book was finally published I spotted six
typos on the first page! This was after eighteen
people had read the book. More often than not,
you're going to end up with at least a few errors
in your book. It's not the end of the world.

As a famous marketer once said "Money Loves
Speed." If you get hung up on perfection you kill
your momentum and destroy your ability to create bigger and better things.

I've had clients who have gone through this exact
process and hardly even edit the transcriptions
before they publish.

And they've hit #1 bestseller status on Amazon
and then gone on to land a tremendous number
of interviews and media appearances.

Your book just needs to be *good enough.*

When a Book Is a Gold Mine

That being said, you do obviously want your book to be as professional as possible. And that's why you will rely on a professional editor to clean it up for you. You may also need to hire a ghostwriter to add transitions. Because sometimes there isn't much of a transition when going from one category of questions to the next.

The ghost writer will add a sentence or paragraph that ties everything together. Your editor will help you clean it up for grammar, structure and flow.

Those two simple things will really going go a long way in cleaning up your book and making it into the quality product that you expect as a professional business person

You can find editors over a whole range of price points. And how polished and how decent you want your book to be will depend on the quality of editor you choose to hire.

This is all a matter of personal preference. My editor charges me about $1000 for every 25,000 words.

You may scoff at that price, thinking it is too low. If you want to hire the PhD literature major from Columbia then yes, of course you are going to pay a lot more. You're probably going to pay $5000, $10,000 or more. The point is, this doesn't need to be an expensive process, nor should it be.

I've had plenty of books edited for under $500 and they were just fine. So when it comes to editing, it is a personal choice. I allow my clients to choose what level of editing they want.

If you're very good at communication, and the way you speak is very eloquent, you are not going to need a really high end editor to work on your book.

If you're uncomfortable with your grammar and the way you talk then go ahead and spend a little more money on the editor.

There are plenty of places to find editors. Upwork.com is the largest and most reliable. The great thing about this platform is that it is a bid-based system.

You post a job and say, "I have a 10,000 word document that I need edited and cleaned up."

Editors will submit bids and say, "This is how much I will charge you to do it."

And the great thing is you're going to get people from all over the world. (You may want to stick with a native English speaker for the best results.)

I have actually found some of my best editors are people from the Philippines who have masters degrees in English. And because the cost of living in the Philippines is so much less compared to many western countries you can find very reasonable rates from people who are very well-educated.

I used to wonder about the ethics of hiring cheap labor from overseas. Yet, one day I had a conversation with a virtual assistant and it changed everything.

For example, I have two editors on my team that I work with consistently. They are stay-at-home moms who used to be English teachers and they just want to stay busy and keep their minds active.

They're willing to do the work for a reasonable rate because it allows them to stay home with their kids and it provides good pay for their location.

In the case of somebody in the Philippines or India, you're actually providing them a really good living.

When I first started looking to outsource a lot admin work I hated to do, I hired someone out of the Philippines. I posted the job and the contractors set the rate of pay.

In the end, the arrangement was for 30 hours a week at $500/month.

On our first day, I had a conversation with her on Skype. I asked her about her salary and what her future goals were, since $500 a month felt quite low to me.

I discovered that she had been born and educated in the United States, although her family lived was from the Philippines. She had also received a Master's Degree in the United States before deciding to move back home with her family.

So for all intents and purposes, she was American. When I asked about her salary and the living expenses in the Philippines, she said, "My dad has worked as a banker for 20 years and he is in middle management. It took him 15 years to get in to middle management. His salary is $450 a month and he works 50-60 hours a week.

You're paying me $500 a month to work 30 hours a week. I'm working half as much as my father and I'm earning more money than him. I'm living a very nice middle class lifestyle in the Philippines on $500 a month."

And that's when the light went off for me. It's not necessarily about the amount money you are paying... it's about the type of lifestyle that the money provides.

I mention this as I know outsourcing is an emotionally charged topic.

My job in writing this book is to provide you with all of the resources and options available to you.

It's up to you to you to determine who, from where and for how much you will hire to help you.

CHAPTER 5

Time to Lay Out
Your Layout

When a Book Is a Gold Mine

When you get to the point where you're happy with your final edit, there are only a few more steps left.

First, you need to get your manuscript laid out and formatted for printing. This is not a necessary step yet it is one that I recommend. The beauty of Amazon is you can take a word document, upload it, put a cover on it and you have a book on Kindle.

The downside is that even though everything looks great in Microsoft Word, when Amazon converts the file for Kindle the formatting will be off. Others will notice this and it will reflect in your reviews.

For example, the very first book I published was released as a paperback and had a great design. I took a PDF of the main file and thought all I had to do was upload the file through the Kinde platform and I would be good to go.

Unfortunately, the PDF was not formatted correctly for an ebook. So when you opened the book on Kindle the layout was a mess. As a result I got a lot of bad reviews.

When you look at that book today it is rated at about 3 stars because there a lot of 1 or 2 star reviews. These reviews aren't about the content of the book; they are all about the formatting. So you want to make sure your book follows the format of what people expect when they read a book.

There are a lot of creative things you can do with your layout, especially if you're the type of person who's visual and likes things to look pretty.

You may want to put a lot of images and graphics in your book. And that's great; anything you can do to keep your reader entertained and interested is definitely the best route to go.

Most books on the market today don't have many images, so you don't have to have them to have a successful book.

So how do you get the book laid out? The easiest way is to use a service like Upwork. It's important here that you be very specific on how you're going to publish the book.

When a Book Is a Gold Mine

My advice is to always lay out your book like you're going to have it printed. Even if you are only going to put your book on Kindle, I still recommend laying it out like a printed version. That way if you ever decide you do want make printed copies, there is not a lot or extra work that needs to be done.

When you post on Upwork you'll want to say something like, "I have a _____ page book that I need to be laid out for printing standards for _____(whichever platform you are publishing with)." The one that we use the most is CreateSpace.com. That's Amazon's publishing arm.

The required layout for CreateSpace is a fairly standard layout and most people are familiar with it. If you lay your book out according to CreateSpace standards, you can take it to almost any printer and they can print the book out for you. So that's why we choose to go that route.

You can also go to Fiverr.com and search "Convert Word into CreateSpace." You'll find a whole bunch of contractors that will be able to convert and lay out your book to CreateSpace standards, and they'll do a decent job for you.

If you want something a little fancier or you want to be more creative with your layout, then Upwork will be the service to stick with. Contractors on Upwork have a tendency to be a bit more graphic design savvy.

Again, it really depends on what the purpose of the book is. If you're just wanting to get the book out as an information piece that builds your credibility then going with Fiverr.com is totally fine.

CHAPTER 6

Best Book Covers Ever

Once your book is transcribed, edited, and laid out, the final piece of the puzzle is to design your book cover. This is one of the most fun aspects of the process because now you get to put the shiny coat of paint on your book.

There are a couple options here: You can go with a low end option or a medium/high end option. We'll cover both, and we'll also talk about some things to look for to make it easy.

You can actually get some amazing book covers done for not a lot of money. The best resource I have found for getting a book cover created is Fiverr.com. And, yes... you can actually get a book cover made for $5 bucks.

Generally, I'll add a few other things on to the order when I get my covers done, so most of my book covers end up costing about $20, and they turn out great. Two other resources for book covers (Upwork and 99designs) are discussed later in this chapter.

There are two different types of covers that you can have made: Flat (like a poster) and Print Cover.

You need a flat cover, as that's all that is accepted by Kindle. Make sure that it's created to kindle-sized formats, as Amazon is very particular about the size of image you use.

The recommended cover dimensions Amazon suggest are: 2820 pixels by 4500 pixels.

This may not mean much to you. It doesn't need to. Just pass the info to your graphic designer and they'll handle it all for you.

You will also need a print-style cover that includes the front, the spine, and the back cover. There are five things that you'll need for you book:

1. Title

2. Sub-Title

3. Back cover copy

4. ISBN (International Standard Book Number

5. Barcode

You can pick up an ISBNs and barcode for about $125 bucks. The best resource I've found is: www.myidentifiers.com/get-your-isbn-now

If you publish through CreateSpace.com, you can actually get your ISBN for free. However, this is Amazon's own system and it drastically limits the type of distribution you can have for your book.

I've actually created a template for you to download. This template reveals a process for how to create a book title and how to create a subtitle. The template also shows the most critical areas of your cover.

The template shows you where to put endorsements, your descriptive copy your bio box, the ISBN and barcode. I also provide several samples of book covers from clients so you can have a visual guide to how everything should look. You can download the sample by going to: **www.SixFigureAuthorClub.com/bookcover-samples**

For print covers, you have several options.

Fiverr.com, Upwork.com, and 99designs.com.

99Designs is a marketplace just for graphic artists, so the design quality is generally much higher. It is also the most expensive. However, this is your brand you're creating so a little extra expense may be worth it.

What I enjoy about 99Designs is that you get a lot of variety to choose from. You are required to pay $300 upfront. Then, you create a job posting about your book including the title, the design elements you want to see, etc.

Graphic designers will then submit designs from you to choose from. It's not uncommon to see 50-60 different designs. You then choose your top five and submit modifications and changes to the designers.

Once the modifications are done you can share the top five designs on your social media to get feed back from others about the designs they like. This is great because you actually get outside feedback on your final choices for the cover.

Finally, you choose the best one and pay the difference between your $300 deposit and the final bill. In my experience, the final fee is around $400 total.

I've found just as high quality of work on Fiverr.com as I have on 99designs.

I use the same designers over and over again because they deliver the quality I need every single time.

The price on Fiverr can be a big advantage.

Rather than just go with one designer, you can hire several and get several different designs. Generally speaking, it's less than $50 to have three different covers designed.

If you want to have a bigger pool and a little higher quality to choose from, then 99designs offers that. I've only used 99designs for one client book; all the rest have been from Fiverr, and they all have turned out just fine.

CHAPTER 7

Easy Publishing for Everyone

When a Book Is a Gold Mine

Now that all the parts of your book are happily put together, it's time to publish. Finally!

Now, if you are like a lot of my clients, you might be asking, "Will people really take me seriously if I self-publish?"

Ten years ago self-publishing wasn't considered a "legitimate" way to become an author. That's simply not the case anymore. It's very similar to the music industry. There have been plenty of music acts in the last ten years who have published directly on the internet, and have made a lot of money, without relying on an established label to produce and promote them.

Justin Bieber, for example, love him or hate him, is basically self-made.

Taylor Swift took control and created the life she has. Early in her career she signed with Warner Brothers. They tried to make her do something she didn't want to, so she went off on her own.

Then there is Lindsey Stirling. In the beginning over forty different record labels turned her down. Not to be deterred, she started making her own music videos. With total creative freedom, her videos and music went viral. She now makes over $6 Million Dollars a year. And all the major labels… the ones who turned her down flat… are begging to work with her.

That's the power of having a celebrity brand.

You have the same opportunity available to you with your own book.

When it comes to the "self-published" vs. "publisher" debate, I have a unique perspective. My first book I published on my own. I signed a publishing deal for my second book and had the pleasure of having it released through an established publishing house. Because of that experience, I can honestly cover the pros and cons of each.

The pros to self-publishing are that you keep most of the profits. When you publish through Amazon or CreateSpace you keep up to 70% of your book sales.

With a traditional publisher, this is far from the case. On my very first book, I actually did get an offer from a publisher.

When a Book Is a Gold Mine

At the time, I didn't know anything about the book-publishing world. All I knew was that once you had a completed manuscript you submitted it to editors and you tried to get them to publish your book. If they could publish your book then your life was made and you lived happily ever after.

It wasn't until I started to get offers for the book that I quickly learned that is not the case at all. If you're a first time author, you will only get about 10% of the *net* profit from the book.

And here's how that is determined: Let's say your book has a retail price of $18. Bookstores will only pay up to 50% of that, which makes the wholesale price $9. The cost to print your book will be $2. That leaves $7. Which means on the sale of an $18 book, you will only get .70 cents! While the publisher keeps $6!

Contrast that with Amazon where you can get closer to $10.

However, as a first time author who wants to work with a publisher today, it gets worse. You are expected to have a large social media following or a large list of email subscribers before a publishing house will look at your work.

And even if you do find a publisher who's willing to take you on their first questions are about your following.

"How big is your Facebook fan page?

"How many Twitter followers do you have?"

"How big is your YouTube following?"

If you have 40-50 000 followers then they might be interested in publishing you.

It's pretty outrageous if you think about it. If you are able to build a following of 50,000+, then you are already very successful. You don't need any help, because you are able to leverage that following in multiple ways.

Yet, that's the point when publishers get really excited. "You're very successful. We'll totally take 90% of your profits to leverage the following you've already built."

When a Book Is a Gold Mine

Don't get me wrong. I know that there are publishing houses that do take risks to work with new authors. Yet it's rare.

My advice: if you do have an audience of more than 10,000 people you don't need a publisher.

You will be able to make far more money publishing on your own.

Plus, in today's literary world if you're a first-time author you're not going to get an advance at all. In fact, many publishers may ask you to cover the cost of the first printing on your own. In other words, you pay them to publish your book and take all of your profits.

It works like this: They see your manuscript, love it and offer to publish you. Yes! You're an "official" author!

However, you read over your publishing contract and it says: "We are going to put your books in Barnes and Nobles. But to do that we've got to have 5000 books and you have to pay for the printing of those 5000 books."

Factor in a $2 price for 5000 books... and you've got a nice sized bill on your hands. And that's if you GET a publishing deal.

In the early 2000's to be self-published was not a good thing. Most people in the book industry would consider you a "hack." No one would take you seriously as an author.

Yet today there are authors who are making millions of dollars from self-published, low priced kindle books. In fact, not to long ago one of the "hacks" had a major publisher beg him to let them publish his next book! Oh, how things half changed...

In some ways, it reminds me of Hollywood. You can be an actor who no one will represent. You work your tail off, finance your own project and become a festival darling and suddenly everyone is fighting over you. In some ways, you only get offered help once you are already successful.

Besides the industry shaming that took place over being self-published, there was still a benchmark that had to be met: it was expensive!

When a Book Is a Gold Mine

Let me share with you the personal experience I had with my very first book back in 2008. Afterwards, I'll compare that to the publishing costs for this book so you can see how far things have come since the Kindle was introduced.

When I wrote my first book you couldn't just publish your book on Amazon like you can today. If you didn't have a book deal with a publisher, you had to go through an independent printing company to get your book listed on the Amazon website.

The process is called a print-on-demand service. When someone goes on Amazon and orders your book, the orders go through these print houses. These printers then print and ship the book out to the buyer as they demand them. Hence, the name.

This was a HUGE advancement because until then the only way to get your book published was to find a printer and print it on your own. And to get the price-per-book down to a reasonable you'd generally have to order 1000+ books. The issue now was that you have a garage full of books!

The advent of print on demand changed the publishing game because now you only needed to print your book as they were ordered.

Today there are still plenty of those services out there. They're marketed as a self-publishing one-stop shop. They'll help you get your book edited, laid out, printed and listed on Amazon, etc. While they're all very nice and lovely to work with they also charge quite a bit of money for those services. And this is taking the cheap route.

On my first book needed some extensive research completed. I hired someone to do that for me and the total cost was $2200. So right out of the gate, before I even started writing, I was $2200 in the hole.

The topic I covered was unique, so I needed some custom graphics created. The custom graphics and book cover cost me $800.

Then I had to hire somebody to help me with the interior layout, which cost me $500. Now I had a book, yet I had no way to print it. I finally found a print-on-demand service that was able to help me get the book set up on Amazon and ready to print. Their fee was $1800.

Then, as I mentioned before, when I published on Kindle there were some problems with the layout. The entire document layout had to be recreated, which was another $500.

Getting the book published was only the beginning. Now I had to promote it.

Following the "proven path" of the book industry I hired a publicist. I found a publicist who said he could help me for $1500/month, which was extremely cheap.

As I found out later, there was a reason it was so cheap: He didn't do anything, so I spent $1500 for nothing. My solution? Do more publicity!

I heard about an event called The Publicity Summit held in NYC. At the summit you meet with over 100 different media contacts, many of who have the power to actually schedule an interview with you on their radio or TV show.

The idea behind the event is that you get direct, face-to-face access to these producers and radio show hosts and everybody who can help you get publicity for your book.

During the event there are also speakers brought in who talk about the best way to get radio interviews, get on TV, sell more books, etc. Of course each one of these people was selling his or her coaching and training programs for an additional $5,000 each.

For me, the event was a total wash. I met with a lot of people, and everybody was very excited about the content of my book and thought I had a great idea. In the end not one interview was scheduled.

The fee for the event was $6500. Airfare to NYC plus the hotel was another $1,700.

If you are keeping track, at this point I had spent well over $13,000.

So, that was my first experience with writing and publishing a book. A very expensive learning experience!

Keep in mind that this was all from going the self-publishing route *without printing a single book.*

Here's another example of what the self-publishing route can look like:

In the spring of 2014 I had a client who I helped publish and creatively market her first book on Amazon Kindle.

She followed the *Answer to All Your Questions* method and also filmed all of her answers so that she was simultaneously creating her marketing content. She had her assistant transcribe everything, and then edited the content herself.

The total cost for her to get a book made was $65 for the layout and $25 for the cover. She choose to publish on Kindle only, as the book was a shorter "intro" to what it was that she did.

After the book was on Amazon, she told her friends and customers, who read the book and left her honest reviews. Once she reached ten reviews, we launched her marketing campaign.

48 hours later she hit #1 on the Amazon bestseller list for her category. And from reaching #1 she was able to increase her rates, gained exposure to a higher level of client and saw her company reach expand.

All that for under $100.

However, there is more to the story.

You see, the exposure she received from that first number one book gained attention from one of the "Big 5" publishers in New York who eventually offered her a "real" publishing deal.

She excitedly took it.

There was a catch though: The publisher required her to pay for the cover design, the layout of the interior and the printing costs for the first 3000 copies of the book.

They would then put her book into book stores nationwide.

The total fee for all of that was $8000.

When a Book Is a Gold Mine

Next, the publishing company also wanted her to have her own custom website just for the book and required her to use their graphic designer and web team at a cost of $2200. She decided she needed a logo for the book, which was another $700.

Now, the publisher did have an editor for the book but she wasn't happy with the end result so she hired her own editor for another $2500.

So, after $13,400 she was a "real" author. And she still hadn't sold one single book.

Of course, the way to remedy that was to hire a publicist. She found a great firm who agreed to come on for "only" $5,000 per month. She eventually negotiated that down to $2,500 but had to sign a guaranteed 3-month agreement, so there went another $7,500.

All total, her "real" book published by a "real" publisher with "real" publicity cost her just over $20,000.

Three months later she had a one paragraph blurb on Time.com. She also had an interview on a local morning radio show. The end result of this crazy publicity blitz? Not one book was sold. But hey, her book is in bookstores!

$100 for a self published bestseller or $20,000 for a "real" book which has still never reached the bestseller status. Which would you choose?

For the record, in my experience and the experience of my clients, Public Relations firms (sometimes called PR firms) and publicists, for the most part, are not worth the fee.

If you are a publicist or a PR firm, please contact me if you feel that you can actually deliver results. I would be more than happy to talk to you.

I have found that most PR firms and publicists don't deliver any sort of trackable results and definitely nothing that can unequivically prove that that books were actually sold from their efforts.

So why did I bring the costs up? I bring up costs because I want you to see how much the game has changed.

When a Book Is a Gold Mine

I want you to see that the self-publishing route that I followed six years ago was practically as expensive as it was to go with a publisher. I also wanted to show you the reality of publishing a book with a traditional publisher.

Most people think, "Oh if I get a publisher, they're going to cover all of the costs." Yet that is hardly the case, especially today.

That being said, with my second book I did go with a publisher. And the publisher did cover the editing, the layout design, the cover, and the printing. However, they didn't do any marketing; the marketing was all up to me.

We'll get into marketing strategies later, but when the book was released, I contacted the publisher and said, "Hey what can you do to help me with marketing?"

Their response was basically what most publicists do: they submit you to places to possibly get interviews on podcasts, internet radio shows and generally outlets that don't have a tremendous amount of reach or impact.

The one resource that I found that did actually result in some interviews was a publication called the Radio and TV Interview Report. (www.RTIR.com).

It's an online newsletter that is mailed out to radio and TV producers. As an author, you can buy an ad for about $2000 for 3 months. I used this service and ended up booking over 30 interviews over a two-month period. (Far more than my client did for her $7500!)

However, I made sure to not do any other marketing during this time. I relied on Radio interviews as my soul source of book promotion so I could track the results. At the end of every interview I was plugged my website and book on Amazon. Then I would watch the sales reports to see how many books I sold. It was very easy to track: A big fat ZERO sales.

So after going through all of that I said to myself, "You know what? Let me take a crack at it."

I used the methods that I'm going to teach you in the next chapter and within in two weeks my book hit #7 on the Amazon bestseller list.

When a Book Is a Gold Mine

My publisher actually called me and said, "What did you do? How did you do that? Can you please teach us what you just did, so we can do this for our other authors?"

And that's when a light went on for me.

My exact thought was "Wait a minute, you're the publisher. Shouldn't you know how to do this? I mean, isn't that the point of your business? If you're a publisher, shouldn't you understand marketing? Shouldn't you know how to create a marketing campaign around your authors that will create a best-selling book?"

The fact that they called me and asked me to just give them everything that I had developed so they could charge their other authors for the service was completely ludicrous to me.

My answer was "No." I spent a lot of time and a lot of money learning how online book marketing worked. So I wasn't just going to go and give my information to them for free.

However. I am going to give it all away to YOU for no cost whatsoever. You're going to learn all of my secrets and take everything I've done to create your own best-selling books. And then you're going to be able to create a market-dominating brand from those books.

Before we do that, let's discuss how easy it is now for you to get published.

There are two different services that Amazon offers. I admit, I'm a little Amazon friendly because, lets face it, Amazon is the Goliath. They have the biggest distribution, they have the biggest global reach, they make it extremely easy to get your book up online and their customer support is second to none.

When you publish with Amazon you need to understand that there are two separate services that they offer: CreateSpace.com for print books; Kindle Direct Publishing for ebooks. (www.kdp.amazon.com)

With Kindle, you can literally take a Word document or PDF and a cover image and upload it to Amazon. Within a day your book is live.

It couldn't be easier.

However, remember earlier that I said if you upload the straight documents sometimes the formatting will get thrown off. There is a quick fix for this.

Hire a graphic designer to lay your book out according to traditional publishing standard. Then convert it into a .mobi file type. (You can find somebody to do that for you on Fiverr or on Upwork).

However, there's an even easier way to do it.

First, publish your book to CreateSpace.com. There is a tiny bit more work involved upfront because you do need to lay your book out to CreateSpace printing requirements, yet it will pay off in the long run.

Once you've got everything laid out and you've got a cover, upload them in your account. Amazon has a quality control team that will go through and check everything for you. If something's wrong, a lot of the times, they'll just go ahead and fix it for you.

If they can't fix it, they'll send you an email saying they can't upload your file and explain the problem you need to fix. Once everything is fixed, they'll publish it. Within about 48 hours it will be up on Amazon for purchase. At that point you can order print copies and have them in your hand within a few short days.

Once everything is uploaded to CreateSpace you'll see a little box that says, "Would you like to publish this on Kindle as well?" Click the box, pay the $79 fee and within a few days your book will also be available on Kindle as well.

When I was just starting out with my publishing company, I would publish on Kindle first and then move over to CreateSpace. However, we were having some issues doing our own conversion from a word document to a .mobi file.

When the book would get on Kindle it had all sorts of funky technical issues. Sometimes the files were not working correctly across the full Kindle platform: i.e. the book would work on Apple Kindle apps and Android Kindle apps but it wouldn't work on the Kindle itself.

When a Book Is a Gold Mine

So now, to avoid that hassle, we start with CreateSpace. Amazon will do the conversion for you. As in most cases… if you want the best result just go directly to the source! They obviously know what they're doing and they will make sure everything works.

I absolutely love the Kindle Direct publishing program. Amazon has created some really amazing marketing tools for you to promote your books.

Jeff Bezos realized that we, as independent authors, don't necessarily have the money to do a huge marketing campaign. We don't have the money to compete with any one of the Big 5 publishers.

He also realized that a lot of us have a social following. We have Instagram followers, Twitter followers, Facebook fans and customer lists. He recognized that there should be a way for us to easily promote our books to those people who are already following us.

In the Kindle Direct program, you can do a special on your book. It's a countdown timer where you can discount the price for a set period of time.

The tool allows you to also email the countdown timer to your customers. It's a great way to say, "Hey, my book is going to be on sale for only $2.50 for the next few days. Get it while you can because when the deal is over the price goes back up to $10."

When the customer clicks on the link and lands on your book page, there's a giant timer up top that shows how much time is left before your special discount sale is over. Also a countdown timer on the page as well.

Another tool they give you is the ability to list your Kindle book for free. This is a great tool if you want to get some good publicity and some good reviews for your book.

Now there are some unscrupulous marketers out there who will tell you if you give enough books away for free, you can be a bestseller." Kindle does have a free bestseller list.

My view on this is that giving away 10,000 copies of your book doesn't make you a best*selling* author… it makes you a best distributing author.

When a Book Is a Gold Mine

You're not really a bestselling author; you're the best giveaway author. In my opinion, you're not really an official best-selling author until your book reaches the top 100 on the Amazon Bestseller list. Later on in this book I will discuss methods that you can use to become a bestselling author on Amazon.

CHAPTER 8

Everything I Know About Creating Best-Selling Books, I Learned From A Drug Dealer

Many of my clients have asked me how I cracked the code to being able to guarantee a bestselling book every single time. At the time of printing for this book the group of marketers that I work with have created over 400 bestselling books.

We have a 100% track record.

The majority of those books have reached #1 in at least one category on Amazon and many of those books have been the #1 best selling book in multiple categories.

So how did I do it?

It started several years ago in my work as a freelance writer and marketing strategist. I was approached by a client who asked me to help him with his memoir.

As I began to ask him questions about the project I discovered that, we'll just call him Jack, was one of the biggest drug runners in the world in the 1970s and 80s. After watching the TV shows and movies that were coming out of Hollywood about the drug dealing business, he was disgusted. They were totally wrong and he wanted to set the record straight.

Now, I don't condone what Jack did and many people have questioned why I would work with someone like him because they find him morally reprehensible. However, regardless of what I think of his past life it was an interesting story.

I looked at Jack's story as really incredible TV. If we were able to create a book first, our chances of selling the material would be strengthened. So I agreed to help him with this book, and I ghost wrote the book.

I never had any intention of it being a bestselling book nor did I even know how to make it one. I just knew how to write a book and get it published.

After the book was published on Amazon I received a phone call from Jack.

It went something like this:

"Hey Travis, this is Jack. How's it going? Good, good. So listen, about my book... I really want this book to be a best seller."

When a Book Is a Gold Mine

And I said, "Oh, that's great but we'd have a to raise a whole of money to make that happen. And even then, that's not something I've ever done."

He was very persistent. He said to me, "Now Travis. I don't think you're hearing me. This book needs to be a best-seller."

I won't lie. I started wondering if working with a former drug dealer had been the best decision. For the record, he was "retired" from the business. He had stopped dealing drugs in the late 80's, had gotten busted in the early 90's and spent about 15 years in jail. So at the time that I was working with him he was in his mid-60's.

That being said... when you're talking to a drug dealer whose life story you have just written you are intimately aware of all the crazy, brutal things that he's done with people and TO people. So when he says he wants a best-selling book and doesn't give you much of an option... well, let's just say you start to get a little nervous.

I realized I only had one choice and that was to figure out how to make Jacks book a bestseller.

If I didn't make that happen life could get very interesting for me.

So I executed a "deep dive" into the internet hoping to find something that we could use to make his book a bestseller. I only slept a few hours a day. I devoured everything I could on how to make a book a bestseller.

I felt like the famous copywriter John Carlton. John Carlton is a master copywriter that created a copywriting method he calls "Gun to the head copywriting." He's had more winning sales letters than just about any other copywriter in history.

Someone once asked him what his secret was. He said that he just imagined that he was sitting in a chair and someone had a gun to his head. He had to make his sales copy so persuasive that it could get someone to stop their busy life, read the letter and buy the product. And if his letter didn't do that then he was going to get killed.

It's a good metaphor. In my case, it felt a little too real.

When a Book Is a Gold Mine

After a couple of months of research and study and several nerve wracking calls with Jack I felt that I knew what to do.

Sort of.

At this point it was all just a huge experiment.

I called Jack and said, "Jack, we're going to do some marketing on the book."

My anxiety eased a bit when he replied, "That's good my friend, that's good."

I launched the campaign on a bright, sunny Tuesday morning. And for the next three days I plotted my escape out of town if it didn't work.

I sat on Amazon refreshing the page every five minutes, just watching.

48 hours into the campaign, nothing.

54 hours later, nothing.

60 hours later, nothing.

64 hours later, nothing.

I was drenched in sweat. My office chair was like a swimming pool. I glanced nervously at my packed suitcase in the corner.

I had made a promise to a former drug lord and everything I've tried was not working. Exhausted and resigned to living a life on the run, I refreshed the page one more time.

And there it was: the book at #88 on the non-fiction bestseller list.

I refreshed the screen twice more before I collapsed into my chair a heap of hysterical laughter and crying at the same time.

I had done it.

I didn't call Jack to tell him right away because I wanted to see what would happen. I watched the book throughout the course of the night. It went higher and higher and higher.

The next morning, about 10 o'clock Jack's time, I called him and told him to get on Amazon. With his own eyes, he was able to get on and see his book.

When a Book Is a Gold Mine

The book eventually reached #18 on the best-sellers list. We didn't crack the Top 10, which is what he ultimately wanted. However, he had never directly told me that. He just said he wanted a bestseller. So we agreed that I'd lived up to my end of the bargain.

That was the beginning. That was how I learned how to market, and guarantee, a bestselling book.

From that point on, I refined my methods. I discovered better and more effective ways of creating a bestselling book. I also rediscovered the old adage: the more do you something, the better you get at it. The last fifteen books that I've personally helped market have all hit #1 on the Amazon bestseller list.

CHAPTER 9

Best Selling Strategies

Now that I've told you the story of how I discovered the best way to market books to ensure a bestseller, let's explore a few strategies that YOU can use. These are some of the secrets to creating a bestselling book that consultants, PR firms, publishers and marketers don't want you to know. (Myself included! This is some of my best stuff!)

As I mentioned earlier, Jeff Bezos realized that you and I don't have the marketing power behind us that the big New York book firms have. And since most independent authors don't have that sort of clout or that kind of money, so he wanted to create a way that would allow any author to effectively promote their book. He also set up a system that will reward you if you're successful in promoting your book.

The technology of today allows you the ability to communicate with so many people. There are people on YouTube that have huge subscriber lists, people on Facebook who have vast followings and people on Twitter and LinkedIn that have these large groups of followers. Some Internet marketers and coaches have customer email lists of 5000 people or more.

It was this realization that led to Amazon creating the tools for you to leverage any advantage that you may have. Because if you're promoting your book to your customers and they come to Amazon to buy it, Amazon makes money from that.

The strategies I'm about to share with you to help you get on the bestseller list are specifically for Kindle books because the market's bigger. In terms of having a physical book in your hand and handing that off as a business card, that's great and it feels good. And we're going to do that too. In terms of becoming a bestselling author more eBooks are sold on Amazon than physical books now.

The first tool you have with Amazon KDP is the ability to set the price to what ever you want. There's also no limit to how often you can change it. You can set the book as high as $3000, or you can set the book as low as .99 cents. This flexible pricing model is your first tool in making your book a bestseller on Amazon.

Bestseller Strategy #1

The strategy with this particular technique can only be used once your book is on the Amazon Kindle. It must already be published, live and people have bought it at the listed price.

When it comes to what to price your book at, it's really up to you. However, I prefer to set the Kindle book price at 50% of the print copy. The easiest way to determine the price of your book is to see what other books are selling that are in your genre or market price. Take the average and set your price to that.

After your book is live, try to get twelve to fifteen reviews. Once you've managed to get a minimum of 12 reviews, lower the price of your book to .99 cents. Now don't worry, we're not going to be doing this forever; it's just a marketing strategy.

After you've reduced the price to .99 cents you're going to do a couple of things.

First, You need to talk to people and let them know that a limited time price drop is coming.

if you have a Facebook following, you can do some pre-marketing a day or two before you lower the price to .99 cents. You can really build up a lot of buzz with a post as simple as, "Hey, my book is coming out. I'd really like your support, and I'm going to lower my price to .99 cents for my loyal fans for 24-hours starting at 9:00 AM Saturday."

If you have an email list, you can send out an email to everyone on your list. If you have Twitter send a tweet about it.

Do the same thing with your friends and family. In fact, this is probably the best place to start when promoting your first book.

The point is that you need to talk to people and let them know that the limited time price drop is coming.

On the day that you reduce the price to .99 cents, send/post a follow up message. And every few hours do another follow up blast to your Facebook group, your email list and your Twitter.

Keep it simple. All you want to do is remind people about this opportunity. Something like this will work: "Hey, for the next 24-hours only, you can get my latest book for .99 cents. Price goes back up at midnight."

From what I've seen from the clients who have made a concerted effort to do this you can and will reach the bestseller list.

Amazon dictates what is popular by what is selling on an hourly basis. So if you get 30 to 40 people to buy your book in an hour, most other books aren't going to have that sort of movement. (Huge authors such as Stephen King, Stephanie Meyers, etc., excluded)

This is where the reward system that we discussed earlier kicks in. Amazon's system will see that your book just sold 30 or 40 copies in the last hour and it will reward you for promoting your book by bumping you up onto the bestseller list.

Why? In a lot of ways, it's similar to the way day trading works. Traders watch the hourly changes in price and leverage small changes frequently. With eBooks, Amazon is able to do the same thing. Based on the sales they can determine that you're promoting.

Amazon has a complicated algorithm behind this. Based on how other books are selling, your efforts may result in you outselling established authors during that time frame. You're legitimately the bestselling author for that time period. Your book appears on the bestseller list and now Amazon brings even more attention to your book from all of the people who see it on the list.

It's the ultimate win-win scenario.

There is a catch when you do this. Amazon doesn't necessarily track all of their bestseller lists. They have lots of genres broken down into insanely specific niches.

For example if you want to create a book on cross-stitching or needlepoint, there's actually a needlepoint, cross stitching genre under the hobby section. And trust me, the people who love cross stitching and needlepoint know exactly where to go to find books on the topic that they're interested in.

So the catch is Amazon will never tell you that your book hit the bestseller list. When you do your marketing campaign you have to watch your position all day long. (Or at least have one of your staff members do it).

Simply pull your book up on Amazon. Then just refresh your screen every few hours. When it pops onto the bestseller list you can get a screen shot of it. That's the only proof you're going to have that your book was there.

I can't emphasize this enough: Amazon will never tell you that your book hit the bestseller list. My first book hit #3 and I never even knew it. One of my friends happened to be doing something at 3:00 AM in the morning and saw my name on Amazon and clicked on it. It was #3 yet I never knew because when I saw it before I went to bed it was at #10.

The question you may have is why does Amazon go to all that effort to update the bestseller list every couple of hours?

It's marketing. It's promotion. They see that you are promoting your book and you're getting a lot of sales. It's a hot item and it's selling a lot more books than others in your genre. So naturally, the algorithm says you are the bestselling book at that point in time.

You will trickle up the list to the point where you're compared with all the other books. This is good news for you because there are a lot of people who get on Amazon and just look at the Top 100 to see what's popular. That's what they use to help them choose which book to purchase next.

Amazon rewards all of your marketing efforts because they are making money at the same time you are. So they are going to be helping get more people to look at your book. And these people, if your title is catchy enough, are going to buy your book.

You have the potential to sell hundreds, if not thousands, of copies of your book just from getting on the bestseller list.

The best part about all of this is that you can use this strategy even if you don't have an email list, a Facebook following, or a Twitter account. As I mentioned earlier, you can do this exact same thing with your family and close friends.

When a Book Is a Gold Mine

In order for this strategy to work there *must* be a very concerted effort on your part. The majority of your book sales need to come with in a 4-6 hour window.

If you only have 25 people buy your book over the course of a day, you're just selling one book an hour. At that point, you're probably not getting enough sales to compete with the other books' sales.

That's not saying that you won't hit the best-selling list. This strategy depends on the number of books in the genre that you are writing in. Depending on the genre you may still hit the best-selling list because there is less competition.

I had one client who was in a very specific niche in education. When we got on Amazon and searched in that niche there were only five other books in that entire category because it was such a specialized field.

When we released her book she was able to get up to #1 in her category simply from having her close friends and family buy the book.

Bestseller Strategy #2

Let's move on to Bestseller Strategy #2. This one will pretty much guarantee that you'll hit the best-seller list.

In complete honestly, after I had a few colleagues review this book I had several of my previous marketing clients, along with a couple of other big publishers, contact me and beg me not to include this.

From a business stand point, they had a very valid point. They have paid a tremendous amount of money for my marketing services. So, out of respect for them, I'm not going to share that in this book.

However, I did get permission from them to do this instead. If you go to my website, **www.ItStartsWithABook.com** you'll see that I'm offering this book for free. I just ask that you cover the postage to send it to you.

When you checkout, you have the option to purchase the audio book. If you buy the audio book when you order your free copy then I will send this "forbidden strategy" to you in a PDF via email. I just ask that you not share it with other people.

This strategy outlines a way that will practically guarantee that your book will become a best-seller.

Bestseller Strategy #3

The final strategy is to hire a company who can do all of the marketing for you. If you have a book already published and you've been struggling to do anything with it, my company has a guaranteed best-seller service.

We do 100% of the marketing for you and guarantee your book will land on the bestseller list in at least one genre.

We are the only marketing service that guarantees your book will become a bestselling book on Amazon.

If you are interested in this service, visit our website at **www.SixFigureAuthorClub.com**

At this point, if you're still thinking, "Writing a book seems so hard," (even though I've just given you the entire process), we also have a book-coaching program.

We work directly with you and walk you through the entire process. You will learn all of tips, tricks and techniques to creating your book in record speed. You will go from a blank page to a fully published book in six weeks or less.

You also get my million-dollar Bestseller Black book. This is my own personal database that contains the contact information for all of the editors, graphic designers people, conversion specialists etc. that we use.

We cover everything from soup to nuts as a part of your coaching program.

You can learn more about this personalized service at **www.SixFigureAuthorClub.com/system**

CHAPTER 10

The Authorpreneur's Business in a Book

As I've stated before... "business as usual" is no longer enough. Especially if you're an entrepreneur. Setting up shop, paying rent and a staff, providing a service to people at your location, running some Groupons and buying some Facebook ads is no longer enough. It may keep you alive, yet you'll struggle to grow.

Every single businessperson and I would argue that every single person, has enough experience to write a book. And as you have read this book, you've been able to see all the different strategies that can be used to not only write your book but make it a best seller as well.

Yet once you have your book, then what?

The book is just a start. Becoming a bestselling author is just the beginning. And there are multiple strategies that you can use going forward.

As I said earlier, we're firmly in a place in today's world here being a bestselling author has more credibility and authority than being a medical doctor. (Remember the story about Deepak Chopra?)

Once you're a bestselling author, doors open for you. Once you write a bestselling book in your field, then you can reach out to the organizations that you belong to and offer to speak. (If speaking is a desire of yours.)

There is no faster way to build a speaking career than to have a bestselling book. I mean, there are thousands of people who would love to speak, and they are sending out resumes and promoting themselves trying to get speaking engagements.

When you can send out your name and your picture, and say, "I'm a _____with a successful practice. I also happen to be a bestselling author on this particular aspect of _____," you immediately go to the top of the field.

This can really help you land keynote speeches at big organizational events. And as you promote your speaking career you will also be promoting your book as well.

This is true for anyone of any profession. If you're a real estate agent and you write the bestselling book on how you sold more houses in a month than anyone in your office, you can then go to any realtor association, and offer to speak at their next event.

It's as simple as saying, "Hey, I'm a realtor. I have a bestselling book on how to close more real estate sales; I'd share what I know at your next event." Then, every year when they have their annual meeting you offer to speak again. In many cases, they'll start inviting you without you having to make the offer.

That's how you get started. It all starts with your book.

Your book is also the beginning of increased business.

Many of you have gone through this process already. You went to my webpage and you saw that I was giving this book away for free. I just asked you to cover the postage.

You also had the option to get the audio book and the forbidden bestseller strategy. After that, I gave you the option to purchse one of my home-study courses. After that, I extended an invitation for you to join the Six Figure Author Club.

The process you went through is called a sales funnel in the marketing world. You can create this exact funnel for yourself. In fact, it's the secret to building 6 and 7-figure income streams from one simple book.

CHAPTER 11

When a Book is a Gold Mine:

The Six-Figure Author System

When a Book Is a Gold Mine

In any business you need leads and customers.

If you attract leads online, then you need something that will entice them to visit your website. This can be a special report, a video, an audio and yes, even a free book. This is called a "lead magnet." It's what attracts new customers to you. It's usually something that you are willing to give away for free.

If you've ever tried a free sample at the grocery store you've experienced a lead magnet. The company offered you a taste in the hopes that you would want the whole thing.

That's what you'll be doing with your bestselling book.

After your lead magnet, you'll offer them something at a low cost. Between $7-$17 is pretty standard. Some marketers call this a "tripwire." I personally think that's a horrible name because a tripwire insinuates a booby trap.

That's not what we're doing to our customers. We're not sabotaging them with booby traps at all. We're offering value and welcoming them into our exclusive club.

So you have a lead magnet that is so appealing that it pulls in the people that you want to do business with. Then you offer something even better for under $10 bucks. It's great way to filter out people and it will save you a lot of time.

The reason for this is simple. If you went through the *Answer to All Your Questions Method* then instead of having to spend an hour with each new client answering all his questions, you can give him a copy of your book as a resource.

Think of the power of using your book in this manner. You not only established your credibility by answering a few of your client's questions, but you gave him something of real value that he can use going forward. You've just created extreme credibility with your new client.

So, how do you structure your online sales funnel?

It starts with your book. You offer it for free or at low cost. My preferred method is to offer your book for free and ask people to cover the postage.

When a Book Is a Gold Mine

You may be thinking "If I'm giving my book away for free, that's really expensive."

And if that's all your doing, you're right: it can get expensive fast.

Before I offer the solution, ask yourself this: how much money are you spending to get leads in your business right now?

Several of my plastic surgeon and attorney clients are spend $250 to $300 per person. And that only includes their name and email address. For them, $10 is a relative bargain.

If you run some Facebook ads it may cost you $30 for each name that comes in. Still a bargain compared to $300 per name.

Here's the secret: If a person buys your book he or she is no longer just a lead. This is someone who's put down money because they're interested in what you have. They've raised their hand as a hot lead.

And 25-30% of those hot leads will buy more from you if you offer it to them.

This is how you build a 6 and 7-figure income stream.

It all starts with your book.

Once someone buys your book you give them the opportunity to buy a more enhanced version of what you offer in that book. (Like the audio version and an unpublished chapter).

Let's take a look at what it takes to create a system like this for yourself.

Six-Figure Sales Funnel Methods

One method to facilitate this is to take the content of your book, and distil it down to it's core essentials. Then you take those core essentials and you create training videos around each one.

Another method is to take the "Cliff Notes" of your book and put them in a PowerPoint. Next, you use a program like ScreenFlow or Camtasia and you record your screen as you read through your notes.

When a Book Is a Gold Mine

Finally, you can record yourself reading through all the sections of your book. For this method you are basically teaching your book live as if someone was sitting with you in your office.

Why do you want to do any of that?

Because when someone buys your book you want to offer them the opportunity to go deeper with your material.

The sequence looks like this:

1. They buy your book for $7-$10

2. You offer them the audio version and an unpublished chapter for $37.

3. Next you offer them your video series for $97.

4. You offer additional products or services for $197-297.

5. You thank them for their purchase.

6. You send them frequent emails to Nurture the relationship with them.

Here's what this would like as a flow chart:

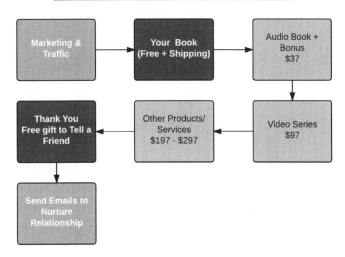

This method could turn a lead that costs you money into a lead that PAYS you money.

Tell me, if your leads paid you to join your club, how many leads would you try to attract? Can you see why this process is so powerful?

If you're still trying to just get your book published, then this may be overwhelming to you. That's OK. You don't need to worry about it right now. Your first priority is to get your book finished.

My purpose is to give you a 30,000-foot view of what's possible from one simple book. Since this may be an entirely new concept to you, let me share some real-life client stories.

The Power of Your Email List

Jon Benson is considered one of the top sales copywriters in the world. He wrote a book that was all about email marketing. He's made tens-of-millions of dollars just by sending emails to his customers.

Most businesses will sell something to their customers, get their email address and then never email that client again. If they do, it's usually not very often. I only hear from my dentist once a year with an email that says "Hey, come in for your check-up." Only emailing your customers once a year is *not* a good way to build your relationship with them.

Building an email list is one of the most powerful, valuable things that any business will ever have because once you have your customers' email, you can send out newsletters, reminders, and other offers to them.

NewYork Times Bestselling author Tracy Hickman has over 6 million fans. When the Internet rolled out he was very resistant to using it. He'd sold millions of books without it. Because of that, he failed to get email addresses from his fans as he travelled the country. Now that everything has moved to social media and email he is playing catch up to get back in touch with his fan base.

The idea using your client emails for marketing may be nauseating. Some of my clients are kind of turned off because in their own words: "I don't want to be a spammer or scammer."

When I look at that and ask: "When people come into your office, are you scamming them? Are you spamming them?" The answer is always no.

To which I reply, "Great, if you're offering a valuable service, why do you not want to offer it to more people?"

I'm sure if you are a chiropractor you have a whole list of products that can make people healthier, lower their inflammation, improve their back pain, and help with their achy joints. However, most of your clients are probably completely unaware of this. Why? Because you're not telling them.

It's fine if you've got a poster on your wall and some brochures because you don't want to be a salesperson. Yet how easy is it to send out a personal email?

Treat it like a message to a close friend. For example, what would you email be to a friend who asked, "What advice can you give me about living a healthier lifestyle?" You would send an email and say, "Here are things that people don't realize. And this is what I personally take to help with these certain issues."

You can do that with your clients. Just send your clients an email and give them the same sort of advice. Include in your email an opportunity for them to buy those things from you. Most of your clients are going to thank you for it and love you for it.

Let's face it, there's always going to be one person that doesn't like what you're doing. If you're afraid to run your business because you don't want one person saying, "I don't like what you're doing," then you might as well get out of business. It doesn't matter what you do, there's always going to be someone who's not happy.

No need for you to waste time or energy on those people. Focus on the people that you can help. If you changed the lives of 37 people for the better with your product or service and one person said, "I'm annoyed because you're sending me two emails a week." Is it worth it? Yes, because you just changed 37 people's lives!

When you give your book away for free, you're getting these people's email addresses so you can follow up with them. You can offer them more services that will enhance their lives.

Let's take a look at Jon. He gives his book away for free. You just cover the postage.

He has also developed some formulas that he uses to compose business emails. This way, he doesn't have to sit down every day and think, "What am I going to write?" He just follows the formula. This formula has generated tens-of-millions for him.

When a Book Is a Gold Mine

His advertisements on Facebook, are simple: "If you want to make money with email, I can help you. In fact, you can get my bestselling book for free."

People click on his ad, come to his page, and pay the postage.

Then, on the next page he has a short video that says:

"Thank you so much for buying my book. It's going to change your life. However, a lot of my clients want to experience results even faster. In my own business I have created email formulas that I follow.

I call them 'The Email Formulas.' These are plug and play, like mathematical equations; you put A here, B here, and it equals C. And C, what does C equal? C equals cash.

Until today, these formulas were only available as part of my $3,000 software. Yet, since you took the initiative and picked up my book, you can get these formulas right now for only $197"

Regardless if they take advantage of his offer or not, on the next page he has a third offer for $297. After that, they are sent to a thank you page.

And of course, he begins to send them emails ever few days offering them other products.

That's how simple your sales funnel can be.

Lets recap:

You start off with your bestselling book, which you sell for a low price.

Before the check out you offer them the chance to add the audio book and a valuable bonus for only $27-$37.

On the next page, you offer them advanced information on the topic of your book for $97-$197. Usually this is videos or an online workshop.

Finally, you make a final offer for a product or service that enhances everything you have offered so far for only $297.

Let's look at another real-world example.

When a Book Is a Gold Mine

You're a plastic surgeon who specializes in surgery-free varicose vein removal. You write a book
on the best ways to remove varicose veins without surgery. Using the power of targeted marketing online, you can run ads to people who would
be interested in this topic.

Once they place the order they are directed to
the next page where you say something like:

"Thank you for purchasing my book. I also have
this product that will reduce the appearance of
varicose veins. It's a skin care cream. You just rub
it on your legs every night before you go to bed
and I guarantee that the sight of your varicose
veins will go down by 90%. You won't even know
they're there. This doesn't remove the hard arter-
ies and veins from your legs yet it does reduce
the appearance of them. You can get this lotion in
my clinic for $197, but add this to your order right
now and its $97 bucks."

If it's related to the problem and your client sees
it as a solution to that problem then they will add
it to the order of your book. On the next page
you thank them have something else you can of-

fer. Finally, you thank them and give them an order confirmation

How to Scale Your Sales Funnel

The way you expand this into a 6 or 7-figure income is to continue to offer products and services. Once someone has raised their hand as being interested when they buy your book, you continue to offer higher end products, such as one-on-one or group coaching, online workshops, retreats, etc.

Now that they've bought your book and a couple of your products you should email them 2-3 times a week. That may seem like a lot yet if you are giving value to your client its not.

Creating three emails a week is not that difficult. It shouldn't take you more than 20 minutes to write an email. You're not writing a novel here. 200-300 words are more than enough.

Here's how to make it even easier: take snippets out of your book and use them as emails.

When a Book Is a Gold Mine

Your first email should say something like this:

"Thank you for requesting your free copy of my bestselling book. I know you're going to love it. What I want you to do is mark this day on your calendar and a month from now I'd like you to write me and tell me how your life has changed from reading my book."

That's the first email. You'll notice that you're not trying to sell anything else to the client at this point. You're simply building rapport..

A couple of days later send a follow up email that says, "Hi, have you gotten my book yet? You may have. If you have, you should really check out page five. Because on page five, I talk about such and such, and here's why this is important to you in your life. Thanks, I'll talk to you later."

In this second email you're helping the client remember the reason that they purchased your book. And you are recommending something that they should read that you feel will help them be successful. Ultimately, this helps him or her remain excited about receiving and reading the book.

A few days later send out a third email. "Hi, it's me again. Did you check out the information on page five? Well you should, because it's really important. Here's why this is important to you and your family…"

However, this time you include a link to an outside article.

"I actually just found this really useful article on md.com that kind of goes into this in more detail,"

Now why did we do that? You're providing value. You just gave them information. When they click on the link and see the high-quality article they will begin to see you as a trusted friend. "Oh man, this article was really helpful. This doctor really cares about me."

It also trains your customers to know that it's okay to click on links in your emails. That's what we want because eventually when you recommend another product of your own or someone else's product and they click on the link, they feel okay doing it because you've proven to them that you're trustworthy.

Another thing that you can include in those first few emails is inviting them to join your blog, your Facebook group where you're posting stuff and to follow you on Twitter

You want your clients to build a trust in what you are sending them. You want to train them to know that it's okay to click on links you send and share your information.

How to Exploit Facebook & Google for Fun and Profit

You have your book. You have your Sales Funnel.

Now it's time to get people to visit your website so they know about your offer.

Just like a store at the local mall, if your website doesn't have anyone stopping by you'll be forced to close shop real soon.

Fortunately for you, there are many, many ways for you to entice highly qualified prospect to visit.

In the online marketing arena, getting visitors to your website is referred to as traffic. The good news is that you can buy all the visitors you could ever want. How you do this?

If you've ever been on Google and done a search you've likely noticed that on the very top it says "ads." Usually the top 3 spaces are highly targeted ads that a company is paying for.

That's why those ads seem to be exactly what you are looking for. It's designed that way to get you to click.

Depending on what you were searching for, the company that placed that ad you just clicked had to pay Google anywhere from $3 to a few hundred dollars. All for one simple click.

The little information pieces you see on the right hand side of the page are all ads as well. Every time you click on one, the business that placed that ad has to pay Google anywhere from a dollar up to several hundred dollars, depending on what the ad is for.

For example, if you search for the KIA Optima in Google and you see an ad at the very top of the page for kia.com, when you click on that ad KIA just paid Google $200-300 for your one click.

Now granted, that's an extreme example. If you decide run Google ads it's good to know that you can set limits on how much you're willing to pay each day in advertising fees. The same process exists for Facebook ads.

Let's say you are a plastic surgeon and you have a book about surgery-free Botox that you want to give away. You decide to run and ad to drive people to get your offer. You put the ad up and you set a limit of $10 a day.

Google or Facebook looks at that and says, "Okay, they're spending $10 a day and this is an offer for people who are interested in Botox." Their algorithm them goes to work that will ensure that your ad appears in front of only people who are interested in Botox.

In other words, the only people who see your ad are the people who are interested in what you're selling. Any time someone sees your ad and clicks on it you have to pay Google or Facebook.

Obviously, not everybody who clicks on your ad and comes to your page is going to buy what you're offering.

So let's say you have a decently converting offer. Conversion simply means out of all the people who visit your website and see your offer, how many buy? For example, let's say that 100 people come to your website but only ten people actually get the book. Your page has a "conversion rate" of 10%.

Now can you see why you can have a $500 sales funnel and the goal is just to break even. Because if 100 people are coming to your website and only ten people buy, then only ten customers will ever see your next offer.

Out of every 100 people who actually see that second offer for $197, maybe only twenty of those are going to buy that. And out of those twenty that go on and see your third offer maybe only eight people are going to buy that.

If you're running your ads on Facebook and it costs you $3 per click, then you will spend $300 for every 100 people who see your website.

When a Book Is a Gold Mine

That's just for them to look at your offer. Yet may only have ten people pick up your book. (There's no profit, as the postage just covers your costs). Out of those ten people maybe only one of them will buy your second offer. At the end of your first day, you've spent $300 and only made $197.

This is where a lot business owners get nervous and stop. They'll spend $300 and they'll only make $200. They'll see that they lost $100 and they immediately shut it down. They will justify their decision with something like: "Oh my God, I'm losing $100. This doesn't work. It's a scam. I'm going to lose all my money. I can't do this."

You have to realize from the beginning, if you want to build a six or seven figure income stream, you will lose a little bit of money as you figure things out. Don't expect to create a massively profitable funnel on your first try.

You've got to figure out what your clients want. You've got to figure out what they will respond to. if you set your daily limit to $5 or $10 over the course of the month, that's only $300. It's slow, yet very worth in in the long run.

If you have the ability to spend $50 a day, which is $1500 in a month, you're going to be able to get to what works faster.

Remember, the goal here is to be able to break even on your ads. Which means that over the course of a month you need to be able to look at your bank account and know that through the little sales funnel you have, you've made at least as much as you've spent on ads.

If you can do the same thing the next month, and the month after that, then you know your funnel is working.

Then you can spend $5000 a month. Why? Because you know you're going to make $5000 back. You can spend $10,000, because you know you're going to make $10,000 back.

Breaking even on your ads is an incredible feeling. Yet, the most value to you is that you're getting customers who are proven buyers. People who buy from you once will most likely buy again.

If you're an attorney, a doctor, in insurance, real estate or other high-ticket service industry you may already be spending $200-300 a lead. You now know a way to create free unlimited leads.

You can build a huge business off of this one simple process. Once you have your leads and your email addresses, what are you doing? You sell them other products.

A Few Real-World Examples

If you're a plastic surgeon chances are that you have services that cost tens-of-thousands of dollars. How often does somebody walk in off the street, meet with you for five minutes and then sign up for a $20,000 procedure?

I'm going to venture not very often.

Using your new Bestselling Book Strategy you create a book using the methods discussed earlier. You offer your solution to a common problem you know many of your patients have. You then create a couple of smaller products, perhaps a skincare line or maybe a $1,000 service that you can offer to clients for $300.

Your funnel in place, you run some ads and entice people to your website where the buy your book. Regardless of whether they buy any of your other offers you've got their emails. Now you can continue to follow up with them.

One of the easiest things to monetize in your funnel at this point is some sort of coaching program. Don't worry, it doesn't have to take a lot of your time. If you create a group-coaching program you can work with dozens of clients in as little as a single hour of your week.

You can send an email that introduces an online anti-aging clinic.

Your email could say something like:

"Hey, I'm going to do a six week anti-aging clinic online. For an hour every week we're going to get together and I'm going to give you the latest techniques, procedures and methods to make your skin look amazing. I'm going to discuss how to reverse the aging process, remove wrinkles, and make you look 15 years younger without Botox or surgery. Normally, an hour consult with me is $1000. However, for this special clinic you'll spend six hours with me for $1,000."

You could have 100 people on the phone, in a webinar or a Google Hangout, all at the same time, and it's still only one hour of your time.

If only ten people take you up on it, that's $10,000. For a six-week program you average $1,666 per hour. Is that worth it to you?

Let's continue the example a little further. You've taken these people to go through your anti-aging program for $1,000 apiece. Now you come up with a $5,000 product. Maybe you have an advanced anti-aging surgical protocol that is a $5,000 service.

Go back to the people who attended your six-week clinic and offer them the chance to get the service before anyone else.

Your email offer could read like this:

"Thank you so much for joining our recent anti-aging clinic. I wanted to let you know about this incredible new technology we acquired. It will easily take 10 years of your face. This cutting edge service has only been available in Europe for $10,000 a treatment. Because you have been such a great customer I want to offer you the opportunity to try this before I let any of my other patients know about it. I'd also like to offer you five treatments for $5000 when you sign up."

Then from there you can come up with a service that's a $10,000 service that would appeal to this demographic.

You now have an online lead generating system that brings you unlimited leads for free and you have all of your higher end services that you can offer them. By doing it this way, it's not going to take you very long before you're making six or seven figures.

All right, so for this example I used a profession that already has high-end services to offer. What if you're not a plastic surgeon? What if you're not a doctor?

The beauty of this strategy is that it doesn't matter what your profession is. Create an offer that your customers want and simply follow the same formula.

If you are a Mortgage Broker you first come up with the idea for your book using the *Answer to All Your Questions* method. In one afternoon you "write" your book using the methods that we discussed earlier. Once you have your book ready you set up your website and promote your book.

When someone comes to your site to buy your book, you offer them your video product that reveals the top 5 ways to save $10,000 or more when buying a house. From there, you might have another product about how they can to lower their mortgage interest by 1%. Perhaps you offer a credit restoration program for customers who don't qualify for a mortgage.

Your offer could look like this:

"I'll reveal the 7 Secrets to a 700 Credit Score that most mortgage brokers are never going to tell you. You get an entire easy-to-follow system on how to clean up your credit and lower the interest you currently pay by at least one full percent, guaranteed. And it's only $300."

After this, you can create a coaching program that walks clients through the entire process of buying a home. You would have specific steps for them to follow and offer to help them navigate the confusing, overwhelming world of mortgage paperwork.

Or, you can do a coaching program for people who are already going through the mortgage process by saying, "Hey I'm going to help you avoid all of the pitfalls of the mortgage industry. I'll reveal how to get the best rates, I'll help you with all of your paperwork and I'll show you the hidden "gotcha" clauses that are in every mortgage contract that your broker hopes you never see. And you can get it all for only $500."

Do you think this would add value to your market place? You bet it would.

So how do you take it to the next level? You can teach a two day seminar on everything real estate investors need to know about the mortgage industry. You could charge $2,000 or more for that and market it towards real estate investors.

When a Book Is a Gold Mine

You could also partner with a friend of yours who is a real estate investor to create a one-on-one real estate mentorship for $15,000+.

You sales funnel would look like this:

1. Someone buys your book

2. You offer the video version of the topics in your book along with some checklists they can follow

3. You offer a homestudy course that expands on your book topic even further.

4. You offer your seminar for $2,000.

5. After providing incredible value at your seminar, you present your Mentorship program.

Or, if you would rather coach a group your offer could be:

We're going to be doing an exclusive online training where we will personally hold your hand through everything. This training will be strictly limited to only five people to ensure that you get maximum one-on-one help from us. We guarantee that you will learn everything you need to know about mortgages and Real Estate Investing. You can bring your deals to us and we will analyse them with you to help you make sure they're good deals. It's only $5,000 for twelve weeks of coaching..."

After you have several people go through your $5,000 or $15,000 training, you can take the most successful students create an even higher, more exclusive offer: A Private Mastermind.

"Hey, we're creating an exclusive private group of investors. We'll meet three times a year. Each time we'll fly into a market and spend one day of masterminding and training with celebrity experts.

On day two we'll drive around and do property tours. On day three we'll bring in outside deals that are too big for one person to handle alone. We'll analyse each deal and if it looks good we'll invest in them as a group.

As a member of this private investor club you will have exclusive access to training, property tours and private deals that most people are never going to see. Membership to join this group is only $25,000 per year."

Masterminds groups like this are very popular. People will pay not for the training or deals… but for the chance to associate and be around other successful people like them.

Okay, we've looked at two professions that each deal with higher end clients and services. What if your profession does not generally make a lot of money? What if you're, say, a Yoga Teacher?" (Nothing against Yoga Teachers. I just don't know any that make very much money)

Most people that I know think Yoga is little more than a series of stretches. So for your first book you could focus on this wildly inaccurate view. (Once again, the *Answer to All Your Questions* method would be particularly useful here.)

In your book you can take the reader beyond stretching and show how it's going to lead to a better lifestyle, better health and a better mental condition. You can also write about how this applies to everyday life. See, there's your book.

Simple.

Your first offer could be a one hour Stress Reducing yoga flow video that you personally developed. It's designed specifically for people who are super stressed out to lower their blood pressure and restore a sense of peace quickly.

Your second offer could be yoga for health. Or maybe it's an anti-aging yoga routine.

To create your additional offers, simply go through all the questions you came up with when you wrote your book. Which of those can be expanded on?

Next, you can add a nutritional component to go along with this new program that gives buyers a month of recipes and some advice on Ayurvedic nutrition. You don't have to be a registered dietician to do this. If you're a yoga teacher you already live a healthy lifestyle so you already know everything you need.

After they're in your funnel start to email them useful content. You send them articles and you point them to cool videos that you know they would enjoy. And then you make an offer of health and wellness coaching.

After that could offer a yoga retreat. You don't have to go very far from where you are to do this. It also doesn't need to be elaborate or long. I recently saw an ad for a 3-Day yoga retreat.

Your offer could say:

"In today's hyper busy world, who has time for a lengthy get away? Yet, you deserve to take a break and to let your body, mind and soul rest and recover. That's why I designed a yoga retreat just for you. It takes place on a Friday, Saturday, and Sunday so you don't have to miss a lot of work. You'll have the chance to relax, reinvigorate your body, enjoy healthy food and conversation."

You could charge $1,000 or $2,000 for that. They have to cover their airfare and their own accommodation.

From there you create a private yoga mastermind that's only for people who really take their yoga practice seriously. You meet three times a year for three or four days in exotic locations.

They pay their airfare and hotel, but you provide all the food and all the training on location. Partner up with experts. Partner up with someone who's really good with nutrition. Partner up with a doctor who's a specialist in anti-aging. Partner up with a spiritual guru. Make them part of this group and you just add more and more credibility. Membership dues could easily be $15,000 to $20,000 a year.

Hopefully by now you're starting to see how easy it is to go from a simple $10 book, to a $25,000 program. I understand that this may be an entirely new world for you. You may even feel that there is no way your clients would ever go from a $10 book to a $25,000 program or mastermind.

I can unequivocally say, "Yes, they will!"

My client who is in the tutoring industry had a client spend over $70,000 in a year for tutoring for his son. All from a $7 eBook.

I even had a client who became a millionaire from two car washes... in a tiny town in central Alaska. She wrote a book about how she went from a housewife to millionaire entrepreneur with car washes.

From the book, she offered a "quick start" home-study course that any one could follow to start their own car wash. Then she offered a $2,000 seminar. At the seminar she offered a $50,000 mentorship where she would personally help you start your own car wash… complete with the building blueprints and access to her wholesale equipment contacts.

From that simple $7 book she has gone on to create an additional high six-figure income stream. *All from self-service carwashes!*

If she can do it YOU can do it.

And there are thousands of business owners who are getting this type of money every day. There are business owners who have high level coaching programs that cost $50,000, $100,000 and even $200,000 a year for one client.

If other people who are not nearly as capable as you can do it, so can you.

CONCLUSION

Since you're reading this book you know the process works. Most likely you visited my website and got this book for free. If you did, you were able to see the additional offers I created specifically for this book.

(If you didn't, you can visit **www.ItStartsWithABook.com**)

And over these coming weeks, you'll be able to observe the follow-up strategy I employ through email. Simply model what I'm already doing.

I know how frustrating it can be if you're a business owner and you hit an income plateau. You throw more money at advertising or SEO or your run a Groupon. And while you may see a small bump in income, eventually things flat line again.

Using the strategies found in this book will allow you to smash through any income ceiling you may have hit and grow your business with customers who are a treat to work with.

When I sat down to edit this book, I took some time to figure out how much money I have spent on marketing seminars, coaching and masterminds to learn these strategies. It was well over $150,000.

I don't mention that to brag. I mention it so you know how committed I am to helping you become even more successful than you are.

So in that context, I would like to give you a free gift.

Once a year I do a special live 3-Day Workshop. I call it the "Six-Figure Author Seminar."

During our time together I will:

- Personally work with you and guide you through these strategies and processes

- Help you figure out what your book should be

- Help you figure out how to structure the book so you can get through it quickly

- Show you the next steps to take to get your book published and your funnel built

When a Book Is a Gold Mine

You could come with a completely blank page and no idea of what you want to do. And by the time you leave you will have the beginnings of your book, plus all the steps you need to take in order to get it fully published.

I will also walk you through the process of how to create higher end products and home study courses from the content of your book. Then I'm going to show you how to go from a $10 book all the way up to a $25,000 service.

Additionally I will take you through a high-level an overview of online marketing principles and how to actually get visitors to your website once you create one.

Finally, you receive a complete flowchart of how a sales funnel should work.

Trust me, this is not an event where you will take a few notes and then leave. You will have a fully completed workbook and guide to take home with you. Along with your own book 80% finished. And there will be a few other special surprises in store to make sure that you are 100% prepared for your success.

The cost for this seminar is $1,997. Past attend-
ees have said it was the most actionable content
they've ever received and worth many times the
price.

Yet, since you have this book, I'd like to gift you a
special ticket.

Just go to **www.TravisCody.com/seminars**

For the latest updates and to learn more about
these strategies and techniques, visit
www.SixFigureAuthorClub.com.

For more information on coaching and our bestseller marketing strategies, visit:
www.SixFigureAuthorClub.com/system

Follow Me For Updates And The Latest Proven Strategies

Facebook: www.TravisCody.com/FB

LinkedIn: www.TravisCody.com/
                LinkedIn

Podcast: www.TravisCody.com/
                SixFigureAuthorShow

Made in the USA
San Bernardino, CA
24 June 2018